Test Yourself for

PROFICIENCY

Susan Morris

•

Alan Stanton

Nelson

Thomas Nelson and Sons Ltd
Nelson House   Mayfield Road
Walton-on-Thames   Surrey
KT12 5PL   UK

51 York Place
Edinburgh
EH1 3JD   UK

Thomas Nelson (Hong Kong) Ltd
Toppan Building 10/F
22A Westlands Road
Quarry Bay   Hong Kong

First published by Thomas Nelson and Sons Ltd 1992

ISBN 0–17–555917–1
NPN 9 8 7 6 5 4 3

Printed in Hong Kong

Acknowledgements

The publishers would like to thank the following for permission to reproduce copyright material. They have tried to contact all copyright holders, but in cases where they may have failed will be pleased to make the necessary arrangements at the first opportunity.

Cambridge University Press for the extract from *The Cambridge Encyclopedia of Language* by David Crystal (page 8)
Andromeda Oxford for the extracts from *Eye to Eye* by Peter Marsh (pages 14 and 20)
Times Books for the extracts from *Past Worlds: The Times Atlas of Archaeology* (pages 26 and 32)
Phaidon Press for the extract from *The Story of Art* (15th edition, 1989) by E. H. Gombrich (page 38)
The Independent for the extract on page 44
Hodder & Stoughton Ltd./New English Library Ltd. for the extract from *The Making of the English Landscape* by W. G. Hoskins (page 50)
Macdonald & Co. for the extract from *Mythology: An Illustrated Encyclopedia* by Richard Cavendish (page 62).

Contents

Notes to the Student

The Cambridge Proficiency in English Examination consists of five papers:

Paper 1 – Reading Comprehension (1 hour)
Paper 2 – Composition (2 hours)
Paper 3 – Use of English (2 hours)
Paper 4 – Listening Comprehension (about 30 minutes)
Paper 5 – Interview (about 15 minutes)

Test Yourself for Proficiency is especially designed for self-access use by students preparing for this examination. It contains ten 'mini tests' in exam format, giving intensive practice in Paper 1, Section A (Reading Comprehension) and Paper 3 (Use of English) excluding the passage for comprehension. The question types in these papers test your vocabulary and knowledge of grammar and structure. After each test you can quickly check your progress by using the Key at the back of the book, which provides answers and guidelines for marking.

How to use this book

Reading Comprehension, Section A
You should answer every one of these multiple choice questions. If you don't know the correct answer, try eliminating the wrong ones. If you really don't know the answer, it is better to guess than to leave the question unanswered.

Use of English, Section A
Question 1: Read the whole passage carefully at least twice before you begin to fill the gaps. Complete each gap with one word only. If you are stuck and aren't sure what to put:

- try thinking about the subject of the text yourself. This may help you to think about appropriate vocabulary connected with the subject;
- look at the grammar of the sentences for clues;
- remember that the missing words may be structural words, such as parts of the verb or prepositions. Consider whether the missing word could be a pronoun, or a conjunction.

Question 2: This question tests your knowledge of grammar. Try to identify what structures are being tested, and remember to look out for additional changes that may be necessary, such as the need for a preposition.

Question 3: This question tests your command of commonly used phrases, often connected with verbs. Think about the situation the words give you, and what sort of language normally occurs there. Check for tenses and spelling.

Question 4: This question tests your knowledge of English phrases and the grammar associated with them. Try to think first of the phrase that is required, and then consider how to change the sentence so that the grammar is correct.

Lastly, it's a good idea to keep a total of your score when you check the answers, so that you can measure your progress as you work through the tests.

Test 1

Reading Comprehension

Choose the word or phrase (A, B, C, or D) which best completes each sentence.

1 General Custer was confident of victory despite being vastly .... by the enemy.
A outnumbered   B outclassed   C overcome   D overtaken

2 Don't tell me you've read *War and Peace* .... !
A yet   B still   C already   D just

3 The ministry refused to .... the figures to the press.
A release   B leak   C show   D add

4 Steve .... his chances of passing by spending too much time on the first question.
A threw out   B threw off   C threw away   D threw in

5 Mr Jones gave his sons some money to .... them up in business.
A get   B set   C put   D make

6 .... comes a time when you have to make a decision and stick to it.
A It   B Therefore   C There   D That

7 James had, ... , saved the manuscript of his first novel from the burning house.
A lastly   B at last   C lately   D at least

8 Mr Nixon refused to answer the questions on the .... that the matter was confidential.
A reasons   B excuses   C grounds   D foundations

9 The lawyer insisted that his client .... never have been arrested in the first place.
A should   B must   C ought   D would

10 As they came under heavy fire, the captain ordered his men to ....
A fall away   B fall back   C fall over   D fall out

11 How voters will react to this latest political scandal .... to be seen.
A is   B remains   C has   D waits

12 'There is no further treatment we can give,' said Dr Jekyll. 'We must let the disease take its ....'
A course   B end   C term   D way

13 He walked from the court a free man, having been .... of murder.
A unconvinced   B discharged   C liberated   D acquitted

14 Michael was the .... force behind the company's rapid expansion.
A managing   B leading   C rising   D driving

15 Can you take .... of the shop while Mr Bentall is away?
A management   B running   C charge   D operation

16 Jack and Christine wondered how the rumours had begun to ....
A disseminate   B spread   C run   D develop

17 The minister made no .... of any further negotiations.
A mention   B comment   C indication   D remark

18 The forecasters take a gloomy .... of the economic future.
A regard   B aspect   C view   D outlook

19 You'd rather speak to him yourself, ... ?
A hadn't you   B didn't you   C wouldn't you   D won't you

20 I wish the neighbours .... making so much noise.
A would stop   B will stop   C stopping   D stopped

21 Mrs Nelson's baby is now two weeks ....
A late   B overdue   C delayed   D expected

22 Every worker gets an extra month's salary as an end-of-year ....
A bonus   B addition   C reward   D donation

23 At the scene of the disaster the Prince said some comforting words to the .... relatives.
A lamenting   B wailing   C complaining   D grieving

24 The soldiers walked cautiously through the .... deserted streets.
A obviously   B apparently   C probably   D hopefully

25 Since he spoke about the subject so indirectly, it was difficult to see what he was ....
A getting at   B getting on   C getting in   D getting up

Use of English

1 *Fill each of the numbered blanks in the following passage with* **one** *suitable word.*

For over two hundred years, scholars have shown an interest in the way children learn to speak and understand their first language. Several small-scale studies were .... (1) out, especially towards the end of the nineteenth century, ... (2) data recorded in parental diaries. But detailed, systematic investigation did not begin .... (3) the middle decades of the twentieth century, when the tape recorder .... (4) into routine use. This made it possible to keep a permanent record of samples of child speech, so that analysts .... (5) listen repeatedly to obscure .... (6), and .... (7) produce a detailed and accurate description.

The problems that have to be .... (8) when investigating child speech are quite different from .... (9) encountered when working with adults. It is not possible to carry out .... (10) kinds of experiments, because aspects of children's cognitive development, ... (11) as their ability to .... (12) attention or to remember instructions, may not be .... (13) advanced. .... (14) is it easy to get children to .... (15) systematic judgements about language – a .... (16) that is virtually impossible below the age of three. Moreover, ... (17) who has tried to make a tape recording of a representative sample of a child's speech .... (18) how frustrating this can be. Some children, it seems, are innately programmed to .... (19) off as soon as they notice a tape recorder .... (20) switched on.

2   *Finish each of the following sentences in such a way that it is as similar as possible in meaning to the sentence printed before it.*

> EXAMPLE: We expect he will arrive by nine o'clock.
>
> ANSWER: He is *expected to arrive by nine o'clock.*

a) I won't agree until Tom's apologised.

Only when ....

b) Please don't use the shower after midnight.

Would you mind ....

c) I agree he's a good worker but I still don't think he should get the job.

Despite ....

d) The residents get very angry when bicycles are left in the hallway.

The residents all wish bicycles ....

e) 'John shouldn't have behaved so badly,' said Janet.

Janet objected ....

f) Anna failed to understand how serious her illness was until she spoke to the doctor.

Not until ....

g) They set off to climb the mountain in spite of the fog.

Although ....

h) I do like carrots, but I don't want to eat them every day.

Much as ....

3 *Fill each of the blanks with a suitable word or phrase.*

    EXAMPLE: 'Would you like some toast?'

                   'No, thank you. I've *had some* already.'

a)   A research project has been set up to find out .... that causes this strange phenomenon.

b)   Inspector Morse questioned ten people, ... could give him any useful information.

c)   It's been raining for hours. I wish .... stop.

d)   Be careful how you start the motor. There's no .... happen.

e)   The police investigation .... eight arrests.

f)   It is quite an easy test, so most students will have .... completing it in twenty minutes.

4 *For each of the sentences below, write a new sentence as similar as possible in meaning to the original sentence, but using the word given. This word* **must not be altered** *in any way.*

    EXAMPLE: It is by no means certain that he was responsible for the crime.
                 questionable

    ANSWER: *It is questionable whether he was responsible for the crime.*

a)   The managing director suggested not appointing any new staff.
      freeze

....

b)   They hate each other intensely.
      sworn

....

c)   There's no need to be so upset about the result.
      shed

....

d) I'd be grateful if you could have a look at these figures.
   cast

....

e) I was pleasantly surprised at the result of the meeting.
   came

....

f) Although he has been very determined, he has never managed to defeat his rival.
   determination

....

g) The arrival time of the plane has been changed to 3.30.
   re-scheduled

....

h) Without his personal assistant John wouldn't know what to do next.
   relies

....

Test 2

Reading Comprehension

Choose the word or phrase (A, B, C, or D) which best completes each sentence.

1 John .... it upon himself to ensure that everyone had satisfactory accommo-
   dation.
   A took   B did   C got   D made

2 Douglas took .... of his meeting with the Prime Minister to argue his case.
   A opportunity   B advantage   C chance   D effect

3 In .... , it was a bad idea to pay him in cash.
   A hindsight   B consideration   C retrospect   D knowledge

4 All things .... , he is the best president we are likely to get.
   A considered   B thought   C taken   D added

5 The minister assured us that there were .... funds for this project.
   A rich   B financial   C ample   D deep

6 This painting stands a good .... of winning the prize.
   A possibility   B chance   C opportunity   D certainty

7 As the election results came through, the Prime Minister .... defeat.
   A declared   B granted   C conceded   D announced

8 After months of getting .... , the detectives began to feel that they were
   onto something.
   A somewhere   B nowhere   C everywhere   D anywhere

9 It is very appropriate that the prize .... go to such a young architect.
   A could   B should   C need   D might

10 The High Street in Cambridge is blocked by a lorry that has .... its load.
   A slipped   B shed   C loosed   D overturned

11 There is more work here than I can .... on my own.
   A cope with   B do with   C make out   D go for

12 In the early years of the twentieth century, several rebellions .... in the
   northern parts of the country.
   A rose up   B turned out   C came up   D broke out

13 Marcus never writes the timetable down. He keeps it in his ....
    A brain   B mind   C head   D heart

14 For a couple of hours after I left the dentist's my jaw was still ....
    A asleep   B unfeeling   C painless   D numb

15 I expect .... the course next year.
    A completing   B to complete   C will complete   D completed

16 Don't tell anyone about this, ... ?
    A do you   B won't you   C will you   D should you

17 The accused .... guilty to all charges.
    A pleaded   B admitted   C said   D confessed

18 Do not .... the driver while the bus is in motion.
    A disturb   B distract   C convert   D interrupt

19 The patient's heart-rate and breathing must be carefully .... during the operation.
    A counted   B monitored   C observed   D supervised

20 'There is no .... of forced entry,' said Inspector Morse.
    A mark   B attempt   C trace   D sign

21 Twenty people were arrested during the demonstration, of .... four were charged with obstruction.
    A who   B whom   C which   D them

22 After eating the apple she threw the .... in the bin.
    A core   B remains   C stones   D centre

23 I didn't learn very much .... my time at that college.
    A during   B throughout   C on   D all

24 The unpaid bills will be .... to next month's account.
    A carried in   B carried on   C carried up   D carried over

25 'We have .... !' said the controller, as the rocket rose into the air.
    A lift-off   B take-off   C uplift   D getaway

Use of English

1 *Fill each of the numbered blanks in the following passage with* **one** *suitable word.*

Clothes have .... (1) basic functions. They protect us from .... (2) of temperature, rain and wind and provide a degree of modesty .... (3) covering our bodies. .... (4) is also important however, is the way clothing transmits messages about the wearer's personality, attitudes, social status, behaviour and group allegiances. Some people are more sensitive to dress signals than others, but there are very few who .... (5) to take clothes into .... (6) at all when forming first .... (7).

To .... (8) in with .... (9) social role and to be .... (10) as a valid actor of your part, you usually have to look the part as well as act the part. .... (11) eccentric managers and executives are .... (12) to dress in jeans and baggy pullovers, but they are very much in the .... (13). Clothes in the professional world are a kind of uniform and unwritten rules prescribe .... (14) standards and styles for everyone in the hierarchy. The .... (15) to be accepted is neither to underdress nor overdress. If .... (16) the rules can be combined with a .... (17) individuality and personal flair, then the .... (18) will be greater. Silk scarves, ties and other items that have no real .... (19) can communicate .... (20) from political allegiance to temperament.

2 *Finish each of the following sentences in such a way that it is as similar as possible in meaning to the sentence printed before it.*

    EXAMPLE: We expect he will arrive by nine o'clock.

    ANSWER: He is *expected to arrive by nine o'clock.*

a) Jack plays football more skilfully than Paul.

    Jack is ....

b) 'Hand over the bag or I'll shoot you!' said the robber to the security guard.

    The robber threatened ....

c) Although Professor Sweet knew a lot about grammar, he couldn't answer the question.

    Despite ....

d) Mrs Fielding is too old to make such a journey.

    Mrs Fielding is so ....

e) I am always short of time.

    I never ....

f) I had only just watered the garden when it began to rain.

    Hardly ....

g) I haven't visited any countries in South America except Venezuela.

    Venezuela is ....

h) We cannot exchange tickets in any circumstances.

    Under ....

3   *Fill each of the blanks with a suitable word or phrase.*

   EXAMPLE: 'Would you like some toast?'

   'No, thank you. I've *had some* already.'

a)   'This   is   your   emergency   signal   beacon,'   said   the   instructor,

   '.. you should not travel in these remote regions.'

b)   Do you have .... anyone involved in this case?

c)   .... I had known that five years ago!

d)   This machine is not .... the purpose for which it was designed.

e)   If so much money has been spent, why is there ....

   for it?

f)   Although   he   has   lived   in   Canada   for   ten   years,   Marino   still

   .... to the cold winters.

4   *For each of the sentences below, write a new sentence as similar as possible in meaning to the original sentence, but using the word given. This word* **must not be altered** *in any way.*

   EXAMPLE: It is by no means certain that he was responsible for the crime.
   questionable

   ANSWER: *It is questionable whether he was responsible for the crime.*

a)   At 3 p.m. the visiting football team had still not arrived.
   sign

   ....

b)   A summary cannot bring out the high quality of this book.
   justice

   ....

c)   He had no idea at all that the police were watching him.
   unaware

   ....

d) Joanne has a rather unsatisfactory relationship with her sisters.
    get

    ....

e) Whatever colour you choose, we can supply it.
    matter

    ....

f) Although he is young, there are several ministers even younger than him.
    means

    ....

g) As a champion swimmer, she will never be better than she is now.
    prime

    ....

h) You must eat less sugar.
    intake

    ....

Test 3

Reading Comprehension

Choose the word or phrase (A, B, C, or D) which best completes each sentence.

1   We need guaranteed financial .... before we can even start the design work.
    A agreement   B backing   C analysis   D plans

2   At this time of year farmers .... their crops and store them for winter.
    A gather   B remove   C pick up   D take in

3   After three weeks the cut on Tom's hand had still not ....
    A cured   B joined   C mended   D healed

4   The cliffs on this part of the coast are being .... by the sea.
    A worn   B eroded   C demolished   D deteriorated

5   Guy was .... the conspiracy because of his friendship with the conspirators.
    A caught in   B taken in   C drawn into   D pulled by

6   While on holiday Walter and Daisy were caught .... a military coup.
    A into   B up in   C with   D out of

7   He is a man .... to the police.
    A known   B familiar   C recognisable   D accountable

8   Attendance at the council meeting was very ....
    A poor   B small   C slack   D limited

9   Anyone .... ticket has been stolen should contact the airline immediately.
    A his   B their   C whose   D which

10   Sally regretted .... the journalist so much.
    A telling   B tell   C to tell   D told

11   Mrs Archer is known .... the finest collection of twentieth century art in private hands.
    A as have   B having   C by having   D to have

12   The police promised him .... from prosecution if he co-operated with them fully.
    A safety   B protection   C immunity   D absolution

13 After their catastrophic defeat the .... of the army made their way back to their mountain strongholds.
A survivors   B remnants   C wounded   D deserters

14 This court deals only with .... crime.
A petty   B trivial   C small   D insignificant

15 In this quiz you have the chance to .... your wits against the most intelligent people in England.
A set   B pit   C try   D sharpen

16 More than thirty people .... evidence to the court during the four-week trial.
A gave   B explained   C produced   D spoke

17 Adam is thought .... at sea.
A to have been killed   B having been killed   C to be killed
D be killed

18 The lawyer claimed that the tests had been carried out by experienced scientists but this is not necessarily ....
A so   B the way   C thus   D the method

19 .... what he says, observe what he does.
A Although   B In contrast   C Contrary   D Never mind

20 It was decided that .... the following Thursday.
A we met   B we would meet   C our meeting   D we will meet

21 Most of the victims died because they .... poisonous fumes.
A suffocated   B inhaled   C inspired   D gasped

22 He .... his life to the skill of the surgeons.
A owes   B keeps   C preserves   D maintains

23 His ideas about the future of the company did not .... with those of the chairman.
A fit   B go along   C tally   D suit

24 .... we understand his reasons, we cannot condone his behaviour.
A Even if   B Only if   C What if   D As if

25 I don't think that this fashion will ....
A catch on   B catch up   C catch out   D catch over

Use of English

1 *Fill each of the numbered blanks in the following passage with* **one** *suitable word.*

Conversations are such common, everyday events that we easily take them for granted and assume that they require no special skills. .... (1) at some time or .... (2), most of .... (3) have had problems talking with other people. You may .... (4) yourself unable to get a .... (5) in edgeways, and feel foolish and inadequate. Sometimes you have to interrupt rudely, and are .... (6) feeling that, to other people, you must .... (7) unpleasantly aggressive. Or .... (8) been desperate to speak, you do not know how to stop and risk .... (9) considered boring.

Everyone sometimes finds it difficult to strike .... (10) conversations. The importance of being able to start conversations is .... (11). To have relationships, you have to meet people and get to know them. To get to know them, you have to talk to them. At some point, ... (12) has to be an opening line, but how do you know what to say? Conversations often begin when one person remarks, 'Beautiful weather, isn't it?' or asks .... (13) other clichéd question. Conversation openers are .... (14) original – the anxiety of .... (15) the first approach is not conducive to creative thought – but .... (16) does not matter. .... (17) does matter is that these openers are recognised .... (18) what they are – attempts .... (19) starting a conversation. The words are unimportant, the .... (20) that they have been spoken is.

2   *Finish each of the following sentences in such a way that it is as similar as possible in meaning to the sentence printed before it.*

     EXAMPLE: We expect he will arrive by nine o'clock.

     ANSWER: He is *expected to arrive by nine o'clock.*

a)   Whenever he passed the prison, Bernard remembered the years he had spent there.

     Bernard couldn't ....

b)   If you buy fifteen tickets for the same performance, you can have a 25 per cent discount.

     Provided fifteen ....

c)   Our profits this year are higher than they have ever been.

     Never ....

d)   It is my opinion that he is the greatest artist of the twentieth century.

     I consider him ....

e)   'I did not remove the money from the safe,' said Peter.

     Peter denied ....

f)   *Macbeth* is the play that I enjoy the most.

     There ....

g)   Nobody remained on the ship after the captain had left it.

     The captain ....

h)   The factory seemed to have been damaged by fire.

     It looked ....

3 *Fill each of the blanks with a suitable word or phrase.*

    EXAMPLE: 'Would you like some toast?'

                  'No, thank you. I've *had some* already.'

a) The judge refused to do what the gangsters asked, ... much money they offered him.

b) Robert had filled the freezer with food, ... we were very grateful.

c) Mr Archer complained that the hotel .... the picture in the brochure.

d) All the robbers .... to ten years in prison.

e) Look at these footprints! He .... come this way!

f) Swimming is a good way of .... yourself fit and healthy.

4 *For each of the sentences below, write a new sentence as similar as possible in meaning to the original sentence, but using the word given. This word* **must not be altered** *in any way.*

    EXAMPLE: It is by no means certain that he was responsible for the crime.
                questionable

    ANSWER: *It is questionable whether he was responsible for the crime.*

a) The inspector showed us four potential health hazards.
drew

    ....

b) Margaret desperately wanted Nigel to return.
longed

    ....

c) Jack failed to keep his promise to help us.
let

    ....

d) Michael is a very poor tennis player.
good

    ....

e) If we tried to force him to repay the debt, we would be wasting our time.
    point

    ....

f) The house is dirty because no one bothers to keep it clean.
    trouble

    ....

g) Sheila was dismissed after only three days.
    sack

    ....

h) The committee decided that the crash was not the pilot's fault.
    blame

    ....

Test 4

Reading Comprehension

Choose the word or phrase (A, B, C, or D) which best completes each sentence.

1 This new instrument is ....B........ us a lot of trouble.
   A working   B giving   C making   D producing

2 If you do not repay the money we will, as a last ....D........ , take you to court.
   A measure   B attempt   C act   D resort

3 At the party conference, the Prime Minister ....A........ backing for his new policies.
   A won   B got   C had   D held

4 The two trains came ....B........ ten metres of collision.
   A just   B near   C within   D almost

5 Mary wanted to give Nigel a present that was a little bit out of the ....A........ .
   A ordinary   B normal   C average   D everyday

6 Most people would ....D........ at the chance of working for that company.
   A dive   B grab   C seize   D jump

7 All but two of the injured were ....B........ from hospital within twenty-four hours.
   A discharged   B released   C sent   D allowed

8 We decided to ....D........ a coin to see who would go first.
   A throw   B pitch   C roll   D toss

9 If you want to know which companies to invest in, George can give you some ....D........ .
   A clues   B hints   C words   D tips

10 He was awarded a medal in ....B........ of his services to the Queen.
   A view   B recognition   C regard   D light

11 The racing-driver climbed out of the wreckage completely ....A........ .
   A unwounded   B intact   C unscathed   D well-preserved

12 The King showed his mercy by ....B........ the rebels' lives.
   A saving   B sparing   C granting   D accepting

13 The banks ....A........ the Government's new proposals on credit control.
   A welcomed   B greeted   C flourished   D cheered

14 The entire machine was ....A........ , taken to another factory and re-assembled there.
   A dismantled   B disconnected   C demolished   D uncoupled

15 At the end of the day the shopkeeper walked to the bank, carrying the day's ....B........ in a special bag.
   A income   B takings   C earnings   D profits

16 I don't need to know the whole story, just give me the ....A........ .
   A gist   B details   C essence   D summary

17 The company is suspected ....C........ the trade embargo.
   A having broken   B to break   C of breaking   D breaking

18 ....D........ had I left the hotel when I was surrounded by photographers.
   A No sooner   B Immediately   C Just   D Hardly

19 The rocks in this area have been ....B........ into strange shapes by the wind and rain.
   A broken   B eroded   C moulded   D deteriorated

20 You must refrain ....B........ tea or coffee while taking this medicine.
   A to drink   B from drinking   C drink   D drinking

21 When both parents went to prison, social workers took the children ....C........ care.
   A with   B for   C into   D to

22 William is an authority ....A........ medieval tapestries.
   A on   B with   C about   D in

23 Many of his best photographs of the conflict were taken when he was actually ....B........ fire.
   A on   B under   C in   D to

24 The machine should have switched itself off but it failed to do ....D........ .
   A it   B thus   C that   D so

25 ....D........ we need to complete the repairs is £2,000.
   A Everything   B Only   C Just   D All

22/25

Test Four

Use of English

1 *Fill each of the numbered blanks in the following passage with* **one** *suitable word.*

Aggression has long been a natural feature of human behaviour, perhaps ever since the emergence of the earliest hominids. However, ...there...... (1) is no ......evidence......(2) for organised group conflict before about 12,000 years ago. The development of ......such...... (3) conflict was closely linked to changes ......in...... (4) economy and society, ...and...... (5) probably ......were...... (6) more serious after the adoption of agriculture. Larger populations ......put...... (7) greater pressure on land and resources, and thus increased tension ......between...... (8) neighbours. Settled farmers also had food stores, herd animals and standing crops ......to...... (9) steal. The stresses associated with the emergence of more hierarchical societies ......handled...... (10) over by chiefs and kings may ......also...... (11) have played an important ......role...... (12) in the growth of inter-group conflict.

As human communities became organised into larger units ......the...... (13) warfare they waged became ......even...... (14) more lethal. States had greater resources ......spent...... (15) for aggression, defence and the development of new weapons. The written records of ancient societies tell ......about...... (16) full-time specialists employed by the state to produce armour and weaponry, and expensively-equipped elite forces ......put...... (17) into being. Sometimes the ......area...... (18) social and economic order was moulded around the ......state...... (19) of warfare. The feudal system of medieval Europe, for example, had as ......one...... (20) of its principal objectives, the maintenance of a force of armoured knights.

13/20

2 *Finish each of the following sentences in such a way that it is as similar as possible in meaning to the sentence printed before it.*

      EXAMPLE: We expect he will arrive by nine o'clock.

      ANSWER: He is *expected to arrive by nine o'clock.*

a)   The controller never looked away from the screen.

     At no time ...did the controller look away from the screen

b)   Miranda said she was sorry that she had not read my report yet.

     Miranda apologised ...for not having read my report yet

c)   Only the Chairman's firmness and diplomacy prevented a serious argument between the committee members.

     If ....

d)   You can stay in the flat for free if you pay the bills.

     So long as ....

e)   I didn't mean to be impolite.

     It ....

f)   Despite Jack's strange clothes, everybody ignored him.

     Nobody took ....

g)   It was more of a business arrangement than a marriage.

     It was not ....

h)   You must not communicate in any way with anyone involved in this case.

     You must have ....

3 *Fill each of the blanks with a suitable word or phrase.*

EXAMPLE: 'Would you like some toast?'

'No, thank you. I've *had some* already.'

a) He packed his suitcase the night before .... to be able to leave early the next morning.

b) Dorothy took a packed lunch .... she couldn't get any food on the train.

c) Please make cheques .... Thomas Nelson Ltd.

d) The novel has .... for television by Thomas Smith.

e) When he regained consciousness, he .... himself in hospital.

f) Captain Kidd found the treasure .... many men before him had searched in vain.

4 *For each of the sentences below, write a new sentence as similar as possible in meaning to the original sentence, but using the word given. This word* **must not be altered** *in any way.*

EXAMPLE: It is by no means certain that he was responsible for the crime.
questionable

ANSWER: *It is questionable whether he was responsible for the crime.*

a) Everyone except John will remain on the coach.
apart

....

b) Joan was not sure if it was a good idea to employ such young staff.
misgivings

....

c) £500 is too much to pay for that painting.
worth

....

d) Andrew insisted that the shop gave him his money back.
refund

....

e) Be careful not to waste water.
economical

....

f) The performances take place every two hours.
intervals

....

g) Poverty is only part of the problem.
whole

....

h) James Hogg Ltd. is the only shop that supplies this product.
exclusive

....

Test 5

Reading Comprehension

Choose the word or phrase (A, B, C, or D) which best completes each sentence.

1 George decided to ....A........ from his position as company chairman.
   A step down   B step aside   C step back   D step out

2 The police car drove into the car park and ....B........ sharply.
   A pulled in   B pulled up   C pulled aside   D pulled about

3 The police asked the kidnappers to ....B........ the deadline by six hours.
   A prolong   B extend   C delay   D lengthen

4 You might not get better but this medicine will do you no .....C......... .
   A worse   B danger   C harm   D illness

5 Extra blankets will be supplied on ......A......... .
   A request   B demand   C asking   D need

6 James was ....C........ from school for bad behaviour.
   A exiled   B dismissed   C expelled   D discharged

7 'You are not comparing ....A........ with like,' said Margaret.
   A like   B same   C both   D each

8 The prisoner escaped by ....A........ of a rope ladder.
   A means   B method   C use   D way

9 I could tell that John didn't know ....C........ had been an accident.
   A it   B where   C there   D that

10 ....B........ is understood to be no question of a criminal act having taken place.
   A There   B It   C Although   D And

11 There is nothing we can do ....B........ than wait.
   A except   B other   C rather   D moreover

12 ....B........ no fault of his own, Brian was an hour late for the meeting.
   A From   B For   C By   D Through

13 I've been meaning to ....A........ repairing that fence for ages.
   A get round to   B get out of   C get up to   D get on to

✗ 14 The government decided to ....A........ down on income tax evasion.
A press   (B crack)   C push   D snap

✓ 15 'I don't believe you! You're having me ....B........ !' said Jack.
A out   B on   C over   D up

✗ 16 Over the centuries the feet of many visitors have ....A........ the steps to the castle.
A worn out   B worn through   (C worn down)   D worn in

✗ 17 Everyone on the trip was ....A........ on getting as much out of it as possible.
A determined   (B intent)   C willing   D inclined

✗ 18 They attempted to ....A........ the painting to its original condition.
A restore   B renovate   C repair   D refurbish

✗ 19 The defenders ....C........ the enemy until reinforcements arrived.
(A held off)   B held out   C held away   D held down

✗ 20 As he read the text aloud, the newscaster ....A........ over the words.
A slipped   B twisted   C fell   (D stumbled)

✗ 21 The general was relieved of his command after committing one of the worst ....A........ in the history of warfare.
A faults   B defeats   C disasters   (D blunders)

✓ 22 Check the bottles carefully to make sure they have not been ....B........ .
A broken into   B tampered with   C touched up   D taken out

✓ 23 This is a matter of the ....B........ concern.
A ultimate   B utmost   C utter   D universal

✓ 24 Schoolchildren are gifted at ....B........ nicknames for their teachers.
A developing   B coining   C defining   D hinting

✓ 25 The president declared that time was ....C........ in the search for peace.
A running in   B running through   C running out   D running up

16/25

Test Five

Use of English

1 *Fill each of the numbered blanks in the following passage with **one** suitable word.*

Curiosity about the origins and development of human society is a distinctive feature of our species that can be traced back thousands of years. Even .... (1) ancient times, people kept collections of antiquities from even .... (2) periods. For .... (3) of the human past, archaeology is the only .... (4) of information, as written records are a comparatively recent invention.

Our knowledge of the period stretching back from the present day to the emergence of the first tool-making hominids some 2.5 million years ago .... (5) based predominantly on the remains of settlements, burials and artefacts. It is the .... (6) of these traces that is the domain of archae-ology. From it we .... (7) of the gradual but .... (8) mastery of the environment, beginning .... (9) the first tools, the building of shelters and the knowledge of fire – early .... (10) along a path of successive innovations such as pottery and metallurgy .... (11) has led to the advanced technologies of the present day. We learn also of the change .... (12) hunting and gathering food to keeping animals and planting crops and .... (13) the increasing social complexity which accompanied these developments, eventually .... (14) to the formation of states and empires. The archaeological record of .... (15) recent events is enriched .... (16) the survival of lavishly furnished tombs, temples and palaces which are .... (17) the greatest human cultural and artistic achievements. .... (18) archaeology is not only .... (19) study of the grandiose and spectacular, but also provides evidence of the everyday circumstances of .... (20) people.

32

2 *Finish each of the following sentences in such a way that it is as similar as possible in meaning to the sentence printed before it.*

EXAMPLE: We expect he will arrive by nine o'clock.

ANSWER: He is *expected to arrive by nine o'clock.*

a) His father made him study Latin at the age of three.

At the age of three, he ...*was made to study Latin by his father.*

b) I would prefer you to pay in cash.

I'd rather ...*you paid in cash.*

c) Try as I might, I could not understand the code.

No matter ...*how hard I tried, I could not understand the code.*

d) Professor Helsing knows everything about this manuscript.

There is ...*very much Professor Helsing knows about this manuscript.*

e) If you trade in your existing answerphone, we will reduce the price of a new one by £100.

Trade ...*your existing answerphone and we will reduce the price of a new*

f) Norman was sorry he had lost his temper.

Norman regretted ...*having lost his temper*

g) Although I respect the law, I cannot accept the court's decision.

Much ...*as I respect the law, I cannot accept the court's decision.*

h) Is he the only person who knows the secret?

Does ...*he represent the*

anyone/anybody else know the secret?

12/16

33

3 *Fill each of the blanks with a suitable word or phrase.*

4 ½ / 6

EXAMPLE: 'Would you like some toast?'

'No, thank you. I've *had some* already.'

a) The man who happens to be the ringleader has so far evaded capture.

b) Sonia has only her own greed to blame for what happened.

c) It's an interesting concept but can it be put into practice?

d) If you hadn't seen the policeman, what would you have done?

e) George threatened his neighbour with an axe, for which he received a six-month prison sentence.

f) They hoped that the conference would show a better understanding between nations.

4 *For each of the sentences below, write a new sentence as similar as possible in meaning to the original sentence, but using the word given. This word* **must not be altered in** *any way.*

EXAMPLE: It is by no means certain that he was responsible for the crime.
questionable

ANSWER: *It is questionable whether he was responsible for the crime.*

a) All the other students got their exam results before Maria did.
last

Maria was the last student to get her exam results.

b) When the automatic ticket machines are in operation, there will be no more queues.
put

When the automatic ticket machines are put on, there will be no more queues. into operation,

c) I tried as hard as I could to persuade John not to go.
utmost

I tried my utmost to persuad John not to go.

34

d) What would happen if we refused to pay?
supposing

✓ Supposing we refused to pay, what would happen?

e) Jane is very likely to be promoted.
stands

✓ Jane stands a good chance of being promoted

f) After the lecture, Professor Sweet was exhausted.
left

½ Professor Sweet left the lecture exhausted

g) Mr Keating must report to the police daily until his trial begins.
required

✓ Mr Keating is required to report to the police daily until his trial begins.

h) Bernard never stops complaining.
nothing

✗ Nothing (can) stops Bernard complaining.
Bernard does nothing but complain.

6/8

48½

Test 6

Reading Comprehension

Choose the word or phrase (A, B, C, or D) which best completes each sentence.

1 Tom trains hard, is talented and eager to win – he is, in .... , the perfect competitor.
A total   B whole   C short   D part

2 .... attempts were made to reach those buried beneath the rubble of the collapsed building.
A Strong   B Strenuous   C Energetic   D Exhausting

3 Casinos ensure there is a healthy .... between what they take from gamblers and what they pay out.
A profit   B margin   C difference   D balance

4 He was told that students over the age of twenty-six were not entitled to a government .... to help with their studies.
A handout   B subsidy   C aid   D grant

5 I revised my views .... comments from colleagues.
A in the light of   B further to   C against   D consequent upon

6 He bought the cottage .... renovating it and then selling at a large profit.
A with a view to   B with the target of   C aiming to   D his goal being

7 She got the job .... of considerable competition.
A in the face   B in the teeth   C regardless   D irrespective

8 That is a view to which I do not ....
A agree   B support   C subscribe   D maintain

9 If only he .... help us by talking directly to the boss.
A might   B could   C will   D should

10 It was difficult for the lecturer to .... his voice to the back of the hall.
A shout   B raise   C deliver   D project

11 The dealer .... the cards before the game began.
A mixed   B mingled   C sorted   D shuffled

12 The .... of the pudding is in the eating!
A taste   B proof   C quality   D pleasure

13 After the engine failed, the boat just .... with the current.
   A floated   B moved   C drifted   D rolled

14 The consultant outlined the patient's .... and asked the students to identify the disease.
   A signs   B reactions   C notes   D symptoms

15 Harold would rather we .... hold the meeting on Friday.
   A shouldn't   B weren't to   C didn't   D wouldn't

16 You may not have liked her, but .... be quite so rude?
   A should you   B did you dare to   C did you need to
   D would you have to

17 The company doesn't have a graphics section and .... out all its design work.
   A farms   B sends   C tenders   D offers

18 The politician knew exactly how to call .... a response from the audience.
   A up   B forward   C out   D forth

19 She has not yet got .... her recent illness.
   A by   B through   C over   D out of

20 The new recruits were put under a lot of ....
   A pressure   B worry   C pain   D tension

21 Such a horrible crime created a sense of .... among the public.
   A avenge   B fury   C outrage   D revenge

22 This singer is on the .... of a wonderful career.
   A threshold   B start   C edge   D point

23 Although he was regarded as being a talented actor, his career was not a success in financial ....
   A ways   B terms   C aspects   D points

24 The training manager told the trainees that they would have .... all the techniques needed in selling by the end of the course.
   A mastered   B overcome   C conquered   D vanquished

25 There was .... coverage of the story on all the television channels.
   A complete   B extensive   C total   D absolute

Use of English

1 *Fill each of the numbered blanks in the following passage with **one** suitable word.*

We do not know how art began any more than we know how language started. If we take art to mean .... (1) activities as building temples and houses, making pictures and sculptures, ... (2) weaving patterns, there are .... (3) people in all the world without art. If, on the other .... (4), we mean by art some kind of beautiful luxury, we must realise that .... (5) use of the word is a very recent development and that many of the .... (6) artists of the past never .... (7) of it. We can best understand this difference if we think of architecture. We all .... (8) that there are beautiful buildings and that some of them are true .... (9) of art. But there is .... (10) any building .... (11) the world which was not erected .... (12) a particular purpose. Those .... (13) use these buildings as .... (14) of worship or entertainment, or as dwellings, judge them .... (15) and foremost by the standards of utility. But .... (16) from this, they may like or .... (17) the design or the proportion of the structure. In the .... (18) the attitude to paintings and statues was often similar. We are not .... (19) to under-stand the art of the past if we are quite ignorant of the .... (20) it had to serve.

2   *Finish each of the following sentences in such a way that it is as similar as possible in meaning to the sentence printed before it.*

> EXAMPLE: We expect he will arrive by nine o'clock.
>
> ANSWER: He is *expected to arrive by nine o'clock.*

a)   These are problems which can only be solved politically.

These are problems to which ....

b)   People say that animals are mistreated in that circus, but I didn't see this.

I didn't see ....

c)   If you practise regularly you will become more skilful.

Without ....

d)   Peter's advice to me was to sell the shares immediately.

Peter suggested ....

e)   I am sure the exchange rate will not change.

In my opinion there ....

f)   We can attend the seminar provided we get the manager's approval.

The manager's ....

g)   It sounds very much like a song I heard twenty years ago.

It reminds ....

h)   Sarah thought the traffic warden was a policeman.

Sarah mistook ....

3 *Fill each of the blanks with a suitable word or phrase.*

   EXAMPLE: 'Would you like some toast?'

   'No, thank you. I've *had some* already.'

a) I .... my visit to the dentist but it turned out to be even worse than I had expected.

b) We .... Tom since eight o'clock and he still hasn't arrived.

c) You look upset. What on earth .... ?

d) It .... Sally that you saw; she's in London.

e) I'm tired – I .... getting up so early.

f) Sally .... to come and spend Christmas with us, but she had to change her plans as a result of the bad weather.

4 *For each of the sentences below, write a new sentence as similar as possible in meaning to the original sentence, but using the word given. This word* **must not be altered** *in any way.*

   EXAMPLE: It is by no means certain that he was responsible for the crime.
   questionable

   ANSWER: *It is questionable whether he was responsible for the crime.*

a) I couldn't draw because I didn't have the necessary equipment.
    lack

    ....

b) No special payments have been received by my client.
    receipt

    ....

c) He didn't concentrate on the lecture.
    attention

    ....

d) This car cannot go faster than 60 m.p.h.
    speed

    ....

e) It was unfair that the ice-skater got such low marks.
   deserve

   ....

f) There isn't much that Peter doesn't know about modern art.
   gaps

   ....

g) That painting is nothing like the one I saw at the auction.
   similarity

   ....

h) William remained silent throughout the meeting.
   contribution

   ....

Test 7

Reading Comprehension

Choose the word or phrase (A, B, C, or D) which best completes each sentence.

1 Your son has the .... of a fine musician.
   A beginnings   B makings   C looks   D talents

2 In the .... climate, it is difficult to anticipate what the political reaction will be.
   A current   B topical   C contemporary   D actual

3 People expect their representatives on the council to be ready and willing to .... the important local issues.
   A address   B target   C hit   D criticise

4 The children have such .... appetites that I have to cook them double portions.
   A devouring   B delicious   C voracious   D omnivorous

5 He found that the test was child's ....
   A play   B games   C matches   D delight

6 The teacher is only too .... with the difficulties caused by disruptive students.
   A used   B aware   C familiar   D accustomed

7 Her ability, ... with a determination to succeed, should make her very successful.
   A connected   B coupled   C joined   D related

8 The troops were positioned in .... for action.
   A anticipation   B alert   C standby   D readiness

9 Householders were told not to use hose-pipes as a(n) .... against a serious water shortage.
   A preparation   B precaution   C attempt   D provision

10 The minister received .... a show of support that it was impossible to think he would resign.
   A such   B so   C as   D alike

11 You have failed to pay the outstanding bill and, ..., we have been forced to take the matter further.
   A finally   B consequently   C subsequently   D eventually

12 .... his love of swimming, it's hardly surprising he enjoys spending his holidays by the sea.
   A Recognising   B Given   C Providing   D Granted

13 He's a tough politician – he knows how to .... the storm.
   A ride out   B run down   C keep up   D push back

14 'Relax,' said Harry. 'We're .... the worst.'
   A over   B against   C done with   D finished off

15 Sebastian got .... for damaging his bicycle.
   A ticked off   B browned off   C frightened off   D bitten off

16 He always wants to have things his own ....
   A way   B road   C path   D direction

17 He broke his arm in two places and it was a long time before the bones would
   ....
   A cure   B seal   C knit   D join

18 We couldn't have afforded to buy the house if our parents hadn't helped us to
   .... the cost.
   A pay   B meet   C manage   D achieve

19 John's observation was a bit wide of the ....
   A target   B mark   C point   D goal

20 There are hundreds of endangered .... in the world.
   A species   B breeds   C clans   D varieties

21 The helicopter .... over the ship and lowered a doctor onto the deck.
   A flew   B stationed   C hovered   D stayed

22 Before you start making the pudding, make sure you have all the necessary
   .... ready.
   A food   B pieces   C elements   D ingredients

23 Continue .... the sauce to prevent it sticking to the pan.
   A turning   B moving   C stirring   D agitating

24 Because of the ice, drivers found their cars .... on the road.
   A squealing   B slipping   C squeaking   D skidding

25 The cut on his face needed twelve ....
   A threads   B links   C stitches   D joins

Use of English

1 *Fill each of the numbered blanks in the following passage with* **one** *suitable word.*

When a company discovers it has been defrauded by one of its own computer staff, the question of .... (1) to prosecute is never easily answered. First, the company tries to discover .... (2) the fraud was perpetrated, and to retrace the steps .... (3) the computer programmer responsible. But .... (4) computer systems are .... (5) complex that the .... (6) of pinpointing a single weakness that has .... (7) exploited by a knowledgeable insider is difficult, and sometimes .... (8) economically unrealistic.

Companies rarely .... (9) the police, believing that the resources available to detectives are insufficient to .... (10) with such a crime. Moreover, company directors fear that a police investigation .... (11) disrupt the day-to-day running of the computer department, and, ... (12) news of an inquiry leaked out, the confidence of investors in the company could .... (13) damaged.

The larger and .... (14) successful the crime, the less likely it is that a prosecution will .... (15). If those responsible get caught before they get their hands on the .... (16), they will probably end up in court, but if they .... (17) their tracks and the losses are not discovered until .... (18) later, when the funds have been withdrawn, the chances of a prosecution .... (19) brought are diminished. In some cases, companies .... (20) of bad publicity allow such employees to resign and take with them a good reference.

2 *Finish each of the following sentences in such a way that it is as similar as possible in meaning to the sentence printed before it.*

    EXAMPLE: We expect he will arrive by nine o'clock.

    ANSWER: He is *expected to arrive by nine o'clock.*

a) He threatened the officers with violence.

    He made ....

b) All the children will receive a prize, whatever their score in the competition.

    No matter ....

c) Except for the inspector, everyone was in uniform.

    The inspector was the ....

d) Because of his conviction for fraud, the trainer lost his licence.

    His conviction for fraud ....

e) There has never been a time when the English language was not in a state of change.

    At no time ....

f) Bill found a new job very quickly.

    It didn't ....

g) You'll have to spend at least £500 to get that sort of camera.

    You won't ....

h) Only the managing director and the chief chemist know the details.

    Knowledge ....

3 *Fill each of the blanks with a suitable word or phrase.*

    EXAMPLE: 'Would you like some toast?'

                 'No, thank you. I've *had some* already.'

a)   What a shame the trip .... I was really looking forward to it.

b)   If only you would help, we .... the work in an hour.

c)   I can't offer you any coffee; we seem not to ....

d)   He was wearing dark glasses to .... recognised.

e)   Police .... to take extra care because of the fog.

f)   You can come with me as .... don't make any noise.

4 *For each of the sentences below, write a new sentence as similar as possible in meaning to the original sentence, but using the word given. This word* **must not be altered** *in any way.*

    EXAMPLE: It is by no means certain that he was responsible for the crime.
                questionable

    ANSWER: *It is questionable whether he was responsible for the crime.*

a)   He is certainly not a reliable witness.
    means

    ....

b)   The leader went so fast that no one could keep up with him.
    pace

    ....

c)   Weren't you once the secretary of the Gardening Club?
    use

    ....

d)   We have no use for this equipment.
    nothing

    ....

e) They could not warn people by electronic mail because that might spread the computer virus.
fear

....

f) Martin's habit of taking risks doesn't fit in with his image as a family man.
compatible

....

g) John really must attend the meeting.
crucial

....

h) His whole life was one of deceit and treachery.
throughout

....

Test 8

Reading Comprehension

Choose the word or phrase (A, B, C, or D) which best completes each sentence.

1 Mary said she wanted to be Prime Minister when she grew up but Anna, not to be .... , said she was going to be Queen.
  A overawed   B outdone   C outclassed   D overtaken

2 Sally's remark that she was feeling worn out .... thoughts of a holiday.
  A stimulated   B provoked   C prompted   D engendered

3 The soldiers had little to .... from delaying military action.
  A benefit   B win   C gain   D obtain

4 In terms of protocol, the President takes .... over all others in the country.
  A priority   B the lead   C precedence   D the head

5 In this district there is a growing .... between those with jobs and those without.
  A separation   B fissure   C difference   D divide

6 This champion racehorse is one in a ....
  A hundred   B million   C billion   D thousand

7 I'm not surprised people are arguing – they are at the .... of their tether.
  A end   B limit   C finish   D termination

8 .... you had to find a new job, what would you like to do?
  A Provided   B Supposing   C So   D Though

9 .... from collecting shells, he also enjoys looking for fossils.
  A Except   B Besides   C Apart   D Excluded

10 .... I'm concerned he's the best manager this company has ever had.
  A Where   B As far as   C Whereas   D While

11 To get his proposal accepted, the Finance Manager had to .... heavy pressure from colleagues.
  A fend off   B laugh off   C send off   D push off

12 When attacked by his opponents, the general .... with a strong justification for his policy.
  A hit back   B struck up   C leapt up   D pushed forward

13 Jane's very modest, always .... her success.
   A playing down   B turning around   C keeping down   D pushing back

14 Mark had to .... his pocket money by doing jobs around the house.
   A gain   B work   C earn   D take

15 A .... for the company said that the matter was being investigated.
   A speaker   B representative   C publicist   D spokesperson

16 Activities in the department store were .... by animal rights activists protesting against the sale of fur coats.
   A disorientated   B disrupted   C deranged   D disturbed

17 Farmers decided to .... outside the Ministry of Agriculture in protest against the cut in subsidies.
   A caution   B boycott   C control   D picket

18 The scientist's claim to have visited other planets was greeted with .... laughter from his colleagues.
   A ridiculous   B derisive   C amusing   D ludicrous

19 Opinion polls are conducted in order to .... public attitudes and views.
   A indicate   B calibrate   C gauge   D quantify

20 He's very keen, but has he got the stamina to stay the .... ?
   A race   B course   C length   D championship

21 Any athlete who aims to .... performance by taking drugs is likely to be detected and banned.
   A develop   B enhance   C stimulate   D motivate

22 Tim .... himself as one of the best, if not the best, actors of his generation.
   A estimates   B regards   C appreciates   D values

23 Helen was very much in .... of her father.
   A respect   B awe   C regard   D admiration

24 Stephen felt .... about changing his job.
   A afraid   B apprehensive   C indecisive   D timid

25 Many people .... pleasure in looking after their gardens.
   A derive   B take   C get   D make

Use of English

1 *Fill each of the numbered blanks in the following passage with* **one** *suitable word.*

There are many different ways of looking at a town for the first time. One of them is to walk around it, ... (1) in hand. We may study with our guide-books all the historic, individual .... (2) of a town and get to know .... (3). But then, if we are .... (4) our time and stay to look at the town as a .... (5), other questions begin to .... (6), which even the best guide-books do not answer. Why is the town just .... (7) this, this shape, this plan, this size? Why do its streets run in this .... (8) way, and not in some other way that .... (9) more logical to us?

Here .... (10) the best guide-book fails us. One looks in .... (11) for a book that provides a discussion of the town's physical growth, of .... (12) the original core lay, of the directions in .... (13) it grew, and when and why, and of .... (14) one can account for the street plan that we can see today.

What is the .... (15) of studying towns in this way? For me, it is simply that one .... (16) a greater depth of pleasure out of knowing the anatomy of a town and .... (17) it takes that particular form .... (18) from just considering its superficial features, ... (19) attractive they .... (20) be individually.

2 *Finish each of the following sentences in such a way that it is as similar as possible in meaning to the sentence printed before it.*

    EXAMPLE: We expect he will arrive by nine o'clock.

    ANSWER: He is *expected to arrive by nine o'clock.*

a) Whatever the methods used to obtain the results, drugs were definitely not involved.

    There was no question ....

b) It was the ability to incorporate loan words that made English so rich in vocabulary.

    English became rich in vocabulary ....

c) The Chairman insisted that the Sales Director resign.

    The Sales Director ....

d) The report has still not been written.

    The report has yet ....

e) The latest estimate is that there are six million cats in the UK.

    There are ....

f) Harry pays £50 a week for bed and breakfast.

    Bed and breakfast ....

g) The mistake arose because of inaccurate accounting.

    It was from ....

h) The number of people killed in industrial accidents this year is now fifteen.

    Already this year ....

3   *Fill each of the blanks with a suitable word or phrase.*

   EXAMPLE: 'Would you like some toast?'

   'No, thank you. I've *had some* already.'

a)   Of course I didn't steal the camera – I .... like that.

b)   The climbers were within an hour .... the summit when they were forced to abandon the climb.

c)   There's no need .... ironing the pillow cases.

d)   He criticises his wife .... she does.

e)   If you don't like the job, you .... off resigning.

f)   Why did you get a taxi? I .... a lift.

4   *For each of the sentences below, write a new sentence as similar as possible in meaning to the original sentence, but using the word given. This word* **must not be altered** *in any way.*

   EXAMPLE: It is by no means certain that he was responsible for the crime.
   questionable

   ANSWER: *It is questionable whether he was responsible for the crime.*

a)   When under stress Michael often loses his temper.
   tendency

   ....

b)   His ability to lead seems to come naturally.
   born

   ....

c)   The west of the country suffered worst in the storm.
   bore

   ....

d)   Sally Smith became known throughout the country as a result of her popular TV series.
   household

   ....

e) When estimating the cost of a holiday, it's important to remember all the extra things that add to the cost.
account

....

f) John made his teacher very angry.
incurred

....

g) The committee finally said what they thought of the plans.
verdict

....

h) He used to be a teacher, so he really knows what it's like in the classroom.
firsthand

....

Test 9

Reading Comprehension

Choose the word or phrase (A, B, C, or D) which best completes each sentence.

1 Scottish pound notes are not legal .... in England.
   A tender   B money   C exchange   D value

2 The down and outs under the railway bridge .... stones at the rats to keep
   them away.
   A drove   B beat   C hurled   D struck

3 The tracker stalked the tiger for days but the animal .... capture.
   A missed   B slipped   C jumped   D eluded

4 This book will be a delight to .... readers of science fiction.
   A amateur   B skilled   C seasoned   D loving

5 Christopher is prepared to .... his professional reputation on the idea that
   this stone circle originally had an astronomical purpose.
   A risk   B bet   C gamble   D stake

6 A considerable .... of folklore has built up regarding the magical properties
   of sites such as Stonehenge.
   A pile   B body   C doctrine   D culture

7 You'll be willing to help, ... you?
   A wouldn't   B won't   C shan't   D aren't

8 Let's do our best to help, ... we?
   A will   B should   C shall   D ought

9 .... it not for your help, I would never be able to manage.
   A Were   B Would   C Had   D Should

10 .... for Tom's opposition, we would have agreed to the contract.
   A Be it not   B Would it not have been   C Should it not have been
   D Had it not been

11 The news report .... the plight of the refugees.
   A headlined   B captioned   C highlighted   D pinpointed

12 Many actors go through a .... when their lack of work makes them question their vocation.
A trial   B predicament   C phase   D season

13 It's obvious from the car he drives that John's business is ....
A fine   B wealthy   C vigorous   D booming

14 The sound of the waves .... on the shore lulled her to sleep.
A surging   B thundering   C rolling   D breaking

15 The townspeople formed a .... mob to find and kill the man who killed the sheriff.
A hunting   B lynch   C search   D punishment

16 In any .... period, examples can be found of new words entering the language.
A stated   B given   C named   D certain

17 The two sides are entrenched and any meeting between them is unlikely to .... a result.
A submit   B force   C yield   D concede

18 The old house was unable to withstand the .... of severe winter weather and suffered considerable structural damage.
A extremity   B onslaught   C outrage   D fury

19 Since the information was already in the public .... the newspaper felt free to publish it.
A area   B domain   C eye   D awareness

20 It was a disaster on the .... of the nuclear accident at Chernobyl.
A size   B scale   C terms   D consequences

21 Closure of schools took place .... falling numbers of pupils.
A in the context of   B with regard to   C with a concern for
D in consideration of

22 He works hard, but .... of his health.
A at the expense   B at the limit   C at a cost   D at a loss

23 This type of cheese is very hard to .... by.
A get   B come   C go   D put

24 Doctors are often .... to accidents in rural areas.
A called up   B driven out   C called out   D rung up

25 The Sales Manager spent several months .... up his team.
A drawing   B building   C keeping   D sending

Use of English

1 *Fill each of the numbered blanks in the following passage with* **one** *suitable word.*

Buying at auction is quite different from buying something at a fixed price in a shop. At an auction, it is .... (1) to you to make an offer, called 'a bid', ... (2) what you want to buy. You can bid in two ways. .... (3) you can attend yourself or you can leave your bids with a .... (4) of the salesroom staff. There are two .... (5) in leaving bids: prospective purchasers need not .... (6) their working schedules, and, ... (7), the dangers of bidding unwisely are eliminated.

Auctions usually proceed at a fast .... (8) as the auctioneer uses his skills to control the bidding and identify .... (9) is participating. Signals for bidding .... (10) from person to person, but .... (11) method is used, bids .... (12) be made in as clear and direct a .... (13) as possible. When the bidding stops, the auctioneer may ask 'Any more?' before the hammer is brought down to .... (14) that the sale has been concluded.

After the sale it is normally possible to pay for and collect your .... (15) immediately. Payments may be made .... (16) cash, by .... (17) and at some auction houses by credit card. Buying at auction provides the collector with a rich .... (18) of objects, and represents an .... (19) to build a collection in a manner which can be .... (20) exciting and rewarding.

2 *Finish each of the following sentences in such a way that it is as similar as possible in meaning to the sentence printed before it.*

      EXAMPLE: We expect he will arrive by nine o'clock.

      ANSWER: He is *expected to arrive by nine o'clock.*

a) Some businessmen spend too much time on their work and alienate themselves from their families.

Some businessmen alienate themselves from their families ....

....

b) No one could explain why the money had disappeared.

No one could account ....

c) 'Press the alarm and I'll shoot!' shouted the bank robber to the cashier.

The bank robber ....

d) The course on marketing appeals to me more than the one on finance.

I'd much prefer ....

e) Mary plans to finish her novel and then go abroad immediately.

The moment ....

f) This cough medicine doesn't affect your ability to drive.

This cough medicine has no ....

g) People became aware of the damage to the ozone layer when an enormous hole was discovered over the South Pole.

It was the ....

h) Advanced technology cannot operate without special glass.

Were it not ....

57

3 *Fill each of the blanks with a suitable word or phrase.*

> EXAMPLE: 'Would you like some toast?'
>
> 'No, thank you. I've *had some* already.'

a) I .... to be at a meeting this afternoon, but the snow meant I couldn't get out of the house.

b) His piano playing has improved since he .... two hours a day.

c) The rock star didn't dare leave his hotel .... of being mobbed.

d) The house was so badly damaged in the earthquake that it .... down.

e) They still .... my letter, although I sent it express.

f) The plane .... to arrive at 12.45, so it's already two hours late.

4 *For each of the sentences below, write a new sentence as similar as possible in meaning to the original sentence, but using the word given. This word* **must not be altered** *in any way.*

> EXAMPLE: It is by no means certain that he was responsible for the crime.
> **questionable**
>
> ANSWER: *It is questionable whether he was responsible for the crime.*

a) The committee members said they would remain loyal to the Chairman.
pledged

....

b) The challenger just wasn't talented enough to provide a good contest with the reigning champion.
match

....

c) The worst is over now.
through

....

d) She told Arthur exactly what she thought of what he had done.
   ticking-off

   ....

e) The visitors were very impressed by the gardens.
   impact

   ....

f) He himself admits to a fear of spiders.
   admission

   ....

g) The headmaster has a very good opinion of the physics teacher.
   esteem

   ....

h) The plumber advised me not to use the faulty appliance.
   advice

   ....

Test 10

Reading Comprehension

Choose the word or phrase (A, B, C, or D) which best completes each sentence.

1 I've got just enough time for a word with you, as long as you make it .... and snappy.
   A brief   B short   C curt   D sharp

2 She's clever enough, but if her course lasts for six years, there are those who wonder if she'll go the ....
   A race   B course   C distance   D lap

3 Being alone in the house all day looking after three young children is enough to make anyone's patience wear ....
   A thin   B out   C down   D slim

4 Her training in accountancy provided a sound .... for work in the financial world.
   A footing   B base   C ground   D basis

5 She always fights best when the .... are down.
   A curtains   B chips   C blinds   D supports

6 After years of working together, the partners found themselves .... linked.
   A permanently   B indelibly   C perpetually   D inextricably

7 The President decided to release a number of political prisoners as a(n) .... of goodwill.
   A gesture   B indication   C pledge   D symbol

8 He justified his harsh words on the grounds that they had been made in the .... of the moment.
   A spur   B heat   C flash   D height

9 The company was dealt a .... blow when its chief designer deserted to another firm.
   A killing   B homicidal   C mortal   D suicidal

10 Don't look so worried! You should take the boss's remarks with a .... of salt.
   A teaspoon   B pinch   C grain   D dose

11 Failure to .... with the rules will result in dismissal.
    A assent   B comply   C abide   D consent

12 Rachel has a highly developed .... of fine art.
    A taste   B reaction   C liking   D appreciation

13 Our company has holidays that .... for all tastes.
    A respond   B cater   C suit   D agree

14 The child showed his .... of the food by leaving most of it on his plate.
    A disapproval   B objection   C distaste   D exception

15 Sally has an amazing .... of jokes that she uses to good effect at parties.
    A body   B repertoire   C variation   D store

16 Tania was .... after the accident and had to spend several weeks in bed.
    A injured   B incapacitated   C convalescent   D hampered

17 In the dispute with his neighbour, Mr Smith had a long .... of grievances.
    A recital   B list   C brochure   D file

18 Anna sat on the grass .... an apple.
    A chewing   B munching   C grinding   D sucking

19 Before his act, the magician had to .... an assistant in the audience.
    A use   B conceal   C plant   D locate

20 The bad weather .... longer than had been expected.
    A carried on   B went by   C passed off   D came around

21 After a fall in profits, the company decided to .... the hotel business.
    A pull out of   B back off from   C take out of   D keep away from

22 Jane's been .... a bad patch – a holiday should cheer her up.
    A coming up with   B going through   C putting up with
    D getting down

23 .... do his views reflect those of the company as a whole?
    A To what extent   B In what condition
    C Under what circumstances   D To what end

24 Children are always trying to find out .... they can go with a new teacher.
    A how far   B what length   C what distance   D how long

25 It's .... he was trying to tell us something.
    A as if   B even   C how   D though

Use of English

1 *Fill each of the numbered blanks in the following passage with* **one** *suitable word.*

Interest in mythology has grown steadily throughout the last hundred years, assisted by the realisation that .... (1) are not childish stories or mere pre-scientific explanations of the world, ... (2) serious insights into reality. They .... (3) in all societies, ... (4) the present as well as the past. They are .... (5) of the fabric of human life, embodying beliefs, moulding behaviour and justifying institutions, customs and values.

Myths .... (6) imaginative traditions about .... (7) nature, history and destiny of the world. Definitions of myth .... (8) 'story' fail because a good many myths are not stories at .... (9). The mythology of some .... (10) includes the assignment of different functions to the .... (11) gods and goddesses: one deity presides over agriculture, ... (12) over war and so on. Beyond this, the term myth is also .... (13) to the religious and secular traditions .... (14) exert a powerful influence .... (15) attitudes to life, but the literal accuracy of which there is .... (16) to doubt. .... (17), because myths are woven into the fabric of a society .... (18) they are accepted as true, the impact of new discoveries, new attitudes and new ways of life on myths is usually to undermine them.

When old myths are lost, new ones are needed. No society seems ever to have flourished .... (19) a set of myths containing its vision of its past, its .... (20) and its purposes.

2 *Finish each of the following sentences in such a way that it is as similar as possible in meaning to the sentence printed before it.*

  EXAMPLE: We expect he will arrive by nine o'clock.

  ANSWER: He is *expected to arrive by nine o'clock.*

a) We had to postpone the meeting because of bad weather.

  Bad weather led to the ....

b) You cannot make use of this offer after 15 December.

  This offer is only ....

c) Please don't smoke here.

  I'd rather you ....

d) Peter remembered and so did Mary.

  Peter didn't ....

e) 'You really must explain why the Finance Director acted as he did,' said the Chairman.

  The Chairman insisted on ....

f) I had better leave now.

  It's time ....

g) 'I wasn't the one who falsified the figures,' said the clerk.

  The clerk denied ....

h) Is this the only way we can solve the problem?

  Isn't there ....

3 *Fill each of the blanks with a suitable word or phrase.*

   EXAMPLE: 'Would you like some toast?'

   'No, thank you. I've *had some* already.'

   a) Mary contacted the police because she kept .... by noisy neighbours.

   b) No one was surprised .... She never stayed in any job for more than a few weeks.

   c) It's really cold outside. Don't go out without .... warm.

   d) In the winter she always travels with a spade in the car .... against getting stuck in the snow.

   e) After .... her right knee, the player had to withdraw from the tournament.

   f) The man was arrested as .... tip-off.

4 *For each of the sentences below, write a new sentence as similar as possible in meaning to the original sentence, but using the word given. This word* **must not be altered** *in any way.*

   EXAMPLE: It is by no means certain that he was responsible for the crime.
   questionable

   ANSWER: *It is questionable whether he was responsible for the crime.*

   a) The Member of Parliament did everything he could to exploit the situation.
   advantage

   ....

   b) The villagers prepared themselves to withstand the coming storm.
   braced

   ....

   c) Are you implying that he is a thief?
   infer

   ....

d) The crops were badly affected by the storm.
   effect

   ....

e) All tenants must act in accordance with the regulations about guests.
   comply

   ....

f) He became famous when his first book was published.
   publication

   ....

g) If you want to criticise, then the local authorities are the ones to blame.
   criticism

   ....

h) The authorities had decided they would get tough with dissidents.
   crackdown

   ....

Key

For each test there is a total number of 75 marks. The marks are divided in the following way:

Reading Comprehension
One mark for each correct answer. (Total = 25 marks)

Use of English
Question 1: one mark for each correct answer. Answers must be correctly spelt. No mark will be given if you provide more than one answer. (Total = 20 marks)

Question 2: two marks for each fully correct sentence. One mark if part of the sentence is correct. (Total = 16 marks)

Question 3: one mark for each correct answer. (Total = 6 marks)

Question 4: one mark for each correct answer. (Total = 8 marks)

If you score more than 45 marks on a whole test, you are probably ready to take the examination.

Test 1

Reading Comprehension

1 A
2 C
3 A
4 C
5 B
6 C
7 D
8 C
9 A
10 B
11 B
12 A
13 D
14 D
15 C
16 B
17 A
18 C
19 C
20 A
21 B
22 A
23 D
24 B
25 A

Use of English

1   1   carried
    2   using/analysing
    3   until
    4   came
    5   could
    6   extracts/sounds/utterances
    7   thus/so/finally/thereby
    8   faced/tackled/considered/solved
    9   those
    10 certain/some
    11 such
    12 pay
    13 sufficiently/very/so
    14 Nor
    15 make/express
    16 task
    17 anyone
    18 knows/realises/understands
    19 switch
    20 being

2   a) Only when Tom's apologised will I agree.

    b) Would you mind not using the shower after midnight?

c) Despite the fact that he's a good worker, I don't think he should get the job.

d) The residents all wish bicycles weren't left in the hall.

e) Janet objected to John's bad behaviour/to John behaving so badly.

f) Not until she spoke to the doctor did Anna understand how serious her illness was.

g) Although it was foggy, they (still) set off to climb the mountain.

h) Much as I like carrots, I don't want to eat them every day.

3 a) what it is
b) none of whom; but none of them
c) it would
d) telling what might
e) led to; resulted in
f) no difficulty (in)

4 a) The managing director suggested a freeze on the appointment of new staff.

b) They are sworn enemies.

c) There's no need to shed any tears over the result.

d) I'd be grateful if you could cast an eye over these figures.

e) The result of the meeting came as a pleasant surprise to me.

f) Despite his great determination, he has never managed to defeat his rival.

g) The plane has been re-scheduled to arrive at 3.30.

h) John relies on his personal assistant (in order) to know what to do next.

Test 2

Reading Comprehension

1 A
2 B
3 C
4 A
5 C
6 B
7 C
8 B
9 B
10 B
11 A
12 D
13 C
14 D
15 B
16 C
17 A
18 B
19 B
20 D
21 B
22 A
23 A
24 D
25 A

Use of English

1 1 two/their
2 extremes
3 by
4 What
5 fail
6 account/consideration
7 impressions
8 fit
9 your/a/any
10 accepted/seen/considered/regarded
11 Some
12 able/happy/willing
13 minority
14 certain/the/strict

15 way
16 following/keeping/obeying
17 little/certain
18 effect/result/impression/impact
19 function/utility/purpose
20 anything/everything

2 a) Jack is a more skilful footballer/ football player than Paul./Jack is more skilful at football than Paul.

b) The robber threatened to shoot the security guard if he/she didn't hand over the bag.

c) Despite his (deep/extensive) knowledge of/knowing a lot about grammar, Professor Sweet couldn't answer the question.

d) Mrs Fielding is so old that she cannot make such a journey.

e) I never have enough time.

f) Hardly had I watered the garden when it began to rain.

g) Venezuela is the only country in South American (that) I have visited.

h) Under no circumstances can we exchange tickets/can tickets be exchanged.

3 a) without which
b) any connection/dealings with
c) If only; I wish; Supposing
d) suitable/fit for; being used for; fulfilling
e) so little/hardly anything/nothing to show
f) hasn't got/can't get/isn't used to/accustomed to

4 a) At 3 p.m. there was still no sign of the visiting football team.

b) A summary cannot do justice to (the high quality of) this book.

c) He was quite/completely/totally unaware (of the fact) that the police were watching him/of the police watching him.

d) Joanne doesn't get on (very well) with her sisters./Joanne and her sisters don't get on (very well).

e) It doesn't matter what/No matter what colour you choose, we can supply it.

f) Although he is young, he is by no means/by no means is he the youngest minister.

g) As a champion swimmer, she is in her prime.

h) You must reduce/limit/cut down (on) your intake of sugar/your sugar intake.

Test 3

Reading Comprehension

1 B
2 A
3 D
4 B
5 C
6 B
7 A
8 A
9 C
10 A
11 D
12 C
13 B
14 A
15 B
16 A
17 A
18 A
19 D
20 B
21 B

22 A
23 C
24 A
25 A

Use of English

1 1 Yet/But
2 other/another
3 us
4 find/feel
5 word
6 left
7 seem/appear/sound
8 having
9 being
10 up
11 obvious/clear/undeniable/evident
12 there
13 some
14 rarely/seldom
15 making
16 this/that
17 What
18 for/as
19 at
20 fact

2 a) Bernard couldn't pass the prison without remembering the years he had spent there.

b) Provided fifteen tickets are bought/purchased for the same performance, you can have a 25 per cent discount.

c) Never have our profits been higher than they are this year/as high as they are this year.

d) I consider him (to be) the greatest artist of the twentieth century.

e) Peter denied removing/having removed/that he had removed the money from the safe.

f) There is no play (that) I enjoy more than/as much as *Macbeth*.

g) The captain was the last (person) to leave the ship.

h) It looked as if the factory had been damaged by fire.

3 a) however; no matter how; regardless of how

b) for which

c) did not look like; looked nothing like; looked completely different from; didn't resemble; had faked; had nothing to do with

d) were sentenced

e) must have

f) keeping/getting

4 a) The inspector drew our attention to four potential health hazards.

b) Margaret longed for Nigel to return/for Nigel's return.

c) Jack let us down (by not keeping his promise to help us)./We were let down by Jack.

d) Michael is no good (at all) at tennis.

e) There is no point (in) (wasting our time) trying to force him to repay the debt.

f) The house is dirty because no one takes the trouble to keep it clean./ The reason the house is dirty is that no one takes the trouble to clean it.

g) Sheila got/was given the sack after only three days./They gave Sheila the sack after only three days.

h) The committee decided that the pilot was not to blame for the crash/decided not to blame the pilot for the crash.

Test 4

Reading Comprehension

1	B
2	D
3	A
4	C
5	A
6	D
7	A
8	D
9	D
10	B
11	C
12	B
13	A
14	A
15	B
16	A
17	C
18	D
19	B
20	B
21	C
22	A
23	B
24	D
25	D

Use of English

1
1 there
2 evidence
3 such
4 in
5 and
6 became/grew
7 placed/put/imposed/exerted
8 between/with
9 to
10 ruled
11 also
12 part/role
13 the
14 even/much/ever
15 available
16 of
17 came
18 whole/entire/complete
19 demands/requirements/needs
20 one

2 a) At no time did the controller look away from the screen.

b) Miranda apologised for not having read my report yet.

c) If it hadn't been for the Chairman's firmness and diplomacy/If the Chairman hadn't been firm and diplomatic, there would have been a serious argument between the committee members/a serious argument would have taken place between the committee members.

d) So long as you pay the bills, you can stay in the flat for free.

e) It was not my intention to be impolite.

f) Nobody took any notice of Jack despite his strange clothes.

g) It was not so much a marriage as a business arrangement.

h) You must have no contact/communication with anyone involved in this case.

3 a) in order; so as; because he wanted

b) (just) in case; because/since/as she knew

c) out to; payable to

d) been adapted for

e) found

f) for which

4 a) Everyone apart from John will remain on the coach./Apart from John, everyone will remain on the coach.

b) Joan had misgivings about employing such young staff.

c) That painting is not worth £500/not worth paying £500 for.

d) Andrew insisted on (having/getting/receiving) a refund from the shop/insisted that the shop gave/should give him a refund.

e) Be economical with water./Use water in an economical way.

f) The performances take place at two-hourly intervals.

g) Poverty is not the whole (of the) problem.

h) This product is exclusive to James Hogg Ltd./James Hogg Ltd. is the exclusive supplier of this product.

Test 5

Reading Comprehension

1	A
2	B
3	B
4	C
5	A
6	C
7	A
8	A
9	C
10	A
11	B
12	D
13	A
14	B
15	B
16	C
17	B
18	A
19	A
20	D
21	D

22	B
23	B
24	B
25	C

Use of English

1
1	in
2	earlier
3	most/much
4	source
5	is
6	study
7	learn
8	increasing
9	with
10	steps
11	which/that
12	from
13	of
14	leading
15	more
16	by
17	among
18	Yet
19	the
20	ordinary

2 a) At the age of three, he was made/forced to study Latin by his father.

b) I'd rather you paid in cash.

c) No matter how (hard) I tried, I could not understand the code.

d) There is nothing Professor Helsing doesn't know about this manuscript./There is nothing new/more for Professor Helsing to learn about this manuscript.

e) Trade in your existing answerphone and we will reduce the price of a new one by £100.

f) Norman regretted losing/having lost his temper.

g) Much as I respect the law, I

cannot accept the court's decision.

h) Does anyone/anybody else/any other person/someone/somebody else know the secret?

3 a) thought/known to
b) to blame
c) be put into; work in
d) would you have
e) for which
f) might/would lead to (a)

4 a) Maria was the last student to get her/the exam results.

b) When the automatic ticket machines are put into operation, there will be no more queues./ When the automatic ticket machines are in operation, it will put an end to queues./The automatic ticket machines will put an end to queues.

c) I did/tried my utmost to persuade John not to go.

d) Supposing we refused to pay, what would happen?

e) Jane stands a good chance of being promoted.

f) The lecture left Professor Sweet exhausted.

g) Mr Keating is required to report to the police daily until his trial begins.

h) Bernard does nothing but complain.

Test 6

Reading Comprehension

1 C
2 B

3 B
4 D
5 A
6 A
7 A
8 C
9 B
10 D
11 D
12 B
13 C
14 D
15 C
16 C
17 A
18 D
19 C
20 A
21 C
22 A
23 B
24 A
25 B

Use of English

1 1 such
2 or/and
3 no/few
4 hand
5 this
6 greatest/best/great/famous/ outstanding
7 dreamed/thought
8 know/realise/agree
9 works/examples
10 scarcely/hardly
11 in
12 for
13 who
14 places
15 first
16 apart
17 dislike
18 past
19 likely/able/ready
20 aims/purpose(s)

2 a) These are problems to which there is only a political solution/ the only solution is a political one.

b) I didn't see any animals being mistreated in that circus.

c) Without regular practice, you won't become more skilful.

d) Peter suggested (that) I sold/ should sell/ought to sell the shares immediately.

e) In my opinion there will not be a/will be no change in the exchange rate.

f) The manager's approval is neces- sary/needed before we can attend/ for us to attend the seminar.

g) It reminds me of a song I heard twenty years ago.

h) Sarah mistook the traffic warden for a policeman.

3 a) wasn't looking forward to; was dreading
b) have been expecting/waiting for
c) has happened; is wrong/the matter
d) can't/couldn't have been; wasn't
e) am not used to; hate
f) was going; planned; wanted; was

4 a) I couldn't draw for lack of the necessary equipment.

b) My client is not/has not been in receipt of any special payments.

c) He didn't pay attention to the lecture.

d) This car's maximum speed is 60 m.p.h./This car has a maximum speed of 60 m.p.h.

e) The ice-skater didn't deserve to get such low marks.

f) There are few gaps in Peter's knowledge of modern art.

g) There is no similarity between that painting and the one I saw at the auction.

h) William made no contribution to the discussion at the meeting.

Test 7

Reading Comprehension

1	B
2	A
3	A
4	C
5	A
6	C
7	B
8	D
9	B
10	A
11	B
12	B
13	A
14	A
15	A
16	A
17	C
18	B
19	B
20	A
21	C
22	D
23	C
24	D
25	C

Use of English

1 1 whether
2 how/when
3 of
4 some/most/many
5 so
6 task/job

7 been
8 even/quite/totally/simply/also
9 call/contact/involve/inform
10 deal/cope
11 may/might/could/will/would
12 if
13 be
14 more
15 follow/happen/occur/proceed/
   ensue
16 cash/money/loot
17 hide/cover/conceal
18 much
19 being
20 fearful/frightened/scared/afraid/
   wary

2 a) He made threats of violence against the officers.

b) No matter what they score in the competition/what their score in the competition is, all the children will receive a prize.

c) The inspector was the only person (there) not in uniform.

d) His conviction for fraud cost the trainer his licence.

e) At no time has the English language not been in a state of change.

f) It didn't take Bill long to find a job.

g) You won't get that sort of camera for less than £500.

h) Knowledge of the details is limited/restricted to the managing director and the chief chemist.

3 a) has been/was cancelled/called off; has fallen through; fell through
b) could/would finish/do
c) have any (left)
d) avoid being
e) warned/advised motorists
f) long as you

4 a) He is by no means a reliable witness.

b) The leader set such a fast pace that no one could keep up with him.

c) Didn't you use to be the secretary of the Gardening Club?

d) There is nothing we can do with this equipment.

e) They could not warn people by electronic mail for fear of spreading the computer virus.

f) Martin's habit of taking risks is not compatible with his image as a family man.

g) It is crucial that John attends the meeting.

h) Throughout his life he was deceitful and treacherous.

Test 8

Reading Comprehension

1 B
2 B
3 C
4 C
5 D
6 B
7 A
8 B
9 C
10 B
11 A
12 A
13 A
14 C
15 D
16 B
17 D
18 B
19 C

20 B
21 B
22 B
23 B
24 B
25 B

Use of English

1
1 guide-book
2 features
3 them
4 taking
5 whole
6 arise
7 like
8 particular
9 seems/appears
10 even
11 vain
12 where
13 which
14 how
15 point/purpose
16 gets
17 why
18 than
19 however
20 may

2
a) There was no question of drugs being involved, whatever the methods used to obtain the results.

b) English became rich in vocabulary because of its ability to incorporate loan words.

c) The Sales Director was made/ forced to resign by the Chairman.

d) The report has yet to be written.

e) There are estimated to be six million cats in the UK./There are six million cats in the UK according to the latest estimate.

f) Bed and breakfast costs Harry £50 a week.

g) It was from inaccurate accounting that the mistake arose.

h) Already this year fifteen people have been killed in industrial accidents.

3
a) wouldn't/would never do a thing; am not
b) of reaching
c) to bother/start
d) no matter what; whatever; for everything
e) would be better; are better
f) could/would have given you

4
a) Michael has a tendency to lose his temper when he is under stress.

b) He is a born leader.

c) The west of the country bore the brunt/worst of the storm.

d) Sally Smith became a household name as a result of her popular TV series.

e) When estimating the cost of a holiday, it's important to take account of all the extra things that add to the cost.

f) John incurred his teacher's anger/ wrath.

g) The committee finally gave their verdict on the plans.

h) He has firsthand experience of the classroom.

Test 9

Reading Comprehension

1 A
2 C

3	D
4	C
5	D
6	B
7	B
8	C
9	A
10	D
11	C
12	C
13	D
14	D
15	B
16	B
17	C
18	B
19	B
20	B
21	A
22	A
23	B
24	C
25	B

Use of English

1
1 up/down
2 for
3 Either
4 member
5 advantages
6 interrupt/disturb/alter/change/disrupt
7 secondly
8 pace/rate/tempo
9 who
10 vary/differ
11 whatever
12 should
13 fashion/manner/way
14 indicate/signal/show/confirm
15 purchases/purchase/goods
16 in
17 cheque
18 source/range/variety/selection
19 opportunity
20 both/very/extremely/most

2 a) Some businessmen alienate themselves from their families by spending too much time on their work.

b) No one could account for the disappearance of the money.

c) The bank robber threatened to shoot the cashier if he/she pressed the alarm/warned the cashier that if he/she pressed the alarm, he would shoot.

d) I'd much prefer to do the course on marketing than the one on finance.

e) The moment Mary has finished/finishes her novel, she plans to/will go abroad.

f) This cough medicine has no effect on your ability to drive.

g) It was the discovery of an enormous hole over the South Pole that made people aware of the damage to the ozone layer.

h) Were it not for special glass, advanced technology could not operate.

3 a) am/was supposed/meant; ought; was going
b) started practising
c) for fear; because he was afraid
d) had to be/was pulled/knocked; fell
e) haven't got/received
f) was due/scheduled/expected

4 a) The committee members pledged their loyalty to the Chairman.

b) The challenger was no match for the reigning champion.

c) We are through the worst.

d) She gave Arthur a ticking off.

e) The gardens made a big/considerable impact on the visitors.

f) By/On his own admission, he is afraid of spiders.

g) The headmaster holds the physics teacher in high esteem.

h) The plumber's advice to me was not to use the faulty appliance.

Test 10

Reading Comprehension

1 B
2 C
3 A
4 D
5 B
6 D
7 A
8 B
9 C
10 B
11 B
12 D
13 B
14 A
15 B
16 B
17 B
18 B
19 C
20 A
21 A
22 B
23 A
24 A
25 A

Use of English

1 1 myths
   2 but
   3 exist
   4 of/in
   5 part
   6 are
   7 the
   8 as
   9 all
   10 societies/cultures
   11 various
   12 another
   13 applied
   14 which/that
   15 on
   16 reason/cause
   17 However
   18 where
   19 without
   20 present

2 a) Bad weather led to the postponement of the meeting/the meeting('s) being postponed.

  b) The offer is only available/valid until 15 December.

  c) I'd rather you didn't smoke here.

  d) Peter didn't forget and neither did Mary.

  e) The Chairman insisted on an explanation about/of why the Finance Director had acted as he did.

  f) It's time I left.

  g) The clerk denied falsifying the figures.

  h) Isn't there any other/some other/another way of solving the problem?

3 a) being disturbed/woken up/bothered

  b) when she left/handed in her notice/got the sack

  c) putting on something; wearing something to keep you

  d) as a precaution

  e) injuring/spraining

  f) as a result of a

4 a) The Member of Parliament did everything he could to take advantage of the situation.

b) The villagers braced themselves for the coming storm.

c) Am I to infer that (you think) he is a thief?

d) The storm had a bad effect on the crops.

e) All tenants must comply with the regulations about guests.

f) He became famous on the publication of his first book.

g) If you want to make a criticism, then the local authorities are the ones to blame.

h) The authorities had decided there would be/had decided on a crackdown on dissidents.